This Recipe Book Belongs To:

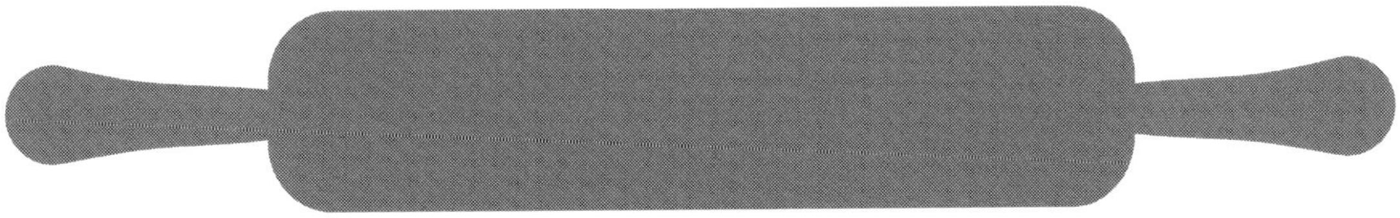

A Collection of
My Favorite Recipes

Table of Contents

Page	Recipe Name

Table of Contents

Page	Recipe Name

Recipe:

Serves: Prep Time: Cook Time: Cook Temp:

Ingredients:

Directions:

Notes:

Recipe:

Serves: Prep Time: Cook Time: Cook Temp:

Ingredients:

Directions:

Notes:

Recipe: ____________________

Serves: ______ Prep Time: ______ Cook Time: ______ Cook Temp: ______

Ingredients:

Directions:

Notes:

Recipe:

Serves: Prep Time: Cook Time: Cook Temp:

Ingredients:

Directions:

Notes:

Recipe: ____________________

Serves: ______ Prep Time: ______ Cook Time: ______ Cook Temp: ______

Ingredients:

Directions:

Notes:

Recipe:

Serves: Prep Time: Cook Time: Cook Temp:

Ingredients:

Directions:

Notes:

Recipe:

Serves: Prep Time: Cook Time: Cook Temp:

Ingredients:

Directions:

Notes:

Recipe:

Serves: Prep Time: Cook Time: Cook Temp:

Ingredients:

Directions:

Notes:

Recipe:

Serves: Prep Time: Cook Time: Cook Temp:

Ingredients:

Directions:

Notes:

Recipe:

Serves: Prep Time: Cook Time: Cook Temp:

Ingredients:

Directions:

Notes:

Recipe:

Serves: Prep Time: Cook Time: Cook Temp:

Ingredients:

Directions:

Notes:

Recipe: ______

Serves: ______ Prep Time: ______ Cook Time: ______ Cook Temp: ______

Ingredients:

Directions:

Notes:

Recipe:

Serves: Prep Time: Cook Time: Cook Temp:

Ingredients:

Directions:

Notes:

Recipe: ______

Serves: ______ Prep Time: ______ Cook Time: ______ Cook Temp: ______

Ingredients:

Directions:

Notes:

Recipe:

Serves: Prep Time: Cook Time: Cook Temp:

Ingredients:

Directions:

Notes:

Recipe:

Serves: Prep Time: Cook Time: Cook Temp:

Ingredients:

Directions:

Notes:

Recipe: ______

Serves: ______ Prep Time: ______ Cook Time: ______ Cook Temp: ______

Ingredients:

Directions:

Notes:

Recipe: ____________

Serves: ______ Prep Time: ______ Cook Time: ______ Cook Temp: ______

Ingredients:

Directions:

Notes:

Recipe:

Serves: Prep Time: Cook Time: Cook Temp:

Ingredients:

Directions:

Notes:

Recipe:

Serves: Prep Time: Cook Time: Cook Temp:

Ingredients:

Directions:

Notes:

Recipe:

Serves: Prep Time: Cook Time: Cook Temp:

Ingredients:

Directions:

Notes:

Recipe: ______________________________

Serves: ________ Prep Time: ________ Cook Time: ________ Cook Temp: ________

Ingredients:

Directions:

Notes:

Recipe:

Serves: Prep Time: Cook Time: Cook Temp:

Ingredients:

Directions:

Notes:

Recipe:

Serves: Prep Time: Cook Time: Cook Temp:

Ingredients:

Directions:

Notes:

Recipe:

Serves: Prep Time: Cook Time: Cook Temp:

Ingredients:

Directions:

Notes:

Recipe:

Serves: Prep Time: Cook Time: Cook Temp:

Ingredients:

Directions:

Notes:

Recipe:

Serves: Prep Time: Cook Time: Cook Temp:

Ingredients:

Directions:

Notes:

Recipe:

Serves: Prep Time: Cook Time: Cook Temp:

Ingredients:

Directions:

Notes:

Recipe:

Serves: Prep Time: Cook Time: Cook Temp:

Ingredients:

Directions:

Notes:

Recipe:

Serves: Prep Time: Cook Time: Cook Temp:

Ingredients:

Directions:

Notes:

Recipe:

Serves: Prep Time: Cook Time: Cook Temp:

Ingredients:

Directions:

Notes:

Recipe:

Serves: Prep Time: Cook Time: Cook Temp:

Ingredients:

Directions:

Notes:

Recipe:

Serves: Prep Time: Cook Time: Cook Temp:

Ingredients:

Directions:

Notes:

Recipe: ______

Serves: ______ Prep Time: ______ Cook Time: ______ Cook Temp: ______

Ingredients:

Directions:

Notes:

Recipe:

Serves: Prep Time: Cook Time: Cook Temp:

Ingredients:

Directions:

Notes:

Recipe:

Serves: Prep Time: Cook Time: Cook Temp:

Ingredients:

Directions:

Notes:

Recipe:

Serves: Prep Time: Cook Time: Cook Temp:

Ingredients:

Directions:

Notes:

Recipe:

Serves: Prep Time: Cook Time: Cook Temp:

Ingredients:

Directions:

Notes:

Recipe: ______________________________

Serves: ________ Prep Time: ________ Cook Time: ________ Cook Temp: ________

Ingredients:

Directions:

Notes:

Recipe:

Serves: Prep Time: Cook Time: Cook Temp:

Ingredients:

Directions:

Notes:

Recipe: ______

Serves: ______ Prep Time: ______ Cook Time: ______ Cook Temp: ______

Ingredients:

Directions:

Notes:

Recipe:

Serves: Prep Time: Cook Time: Cook Temp:

Ingredients:

Directions:

Notes:

Recipe: ______________________________

Serves: ________ Prep Time: ________ Cook Time: ________ Cook Temp: ________

Ingredients:

Directions:

Notes:

Recipe: ____________________

Serves: ______ Prep Time: ______ Cook Time: ______ Cook Temp: ______

Ingredients:

Directions:

Notes:

Recipe: ______________________

Serves: ________ Prep Time: ________ Cook Time: ________ Cook Temp: ________

Ingredients:

Directions:

Notes:

Recipe: ______

Serves: ______ Prep Time: ______ Cook Time: ______ Cook Temp: ______

Ingredients:

Directions:

Notes:

Recipe:

Serves: Prep Time: Cook Time: Cook Temp:

Ingredients:

Directions:

Notes:

Recipe: ______________________________

Serves: ________ Prep Time: ________ Cook Time: ________ Cook Temp: ________

Ingredients:

Directions:

Notes:

Recipe: ______________________________

Serves: ________ Prep Time: ________ Cook Time: ________ Cook Temp: ________

Ingredients:

Directions:

Notes:

Recipe:

Serves: ______ Prep Time: ______ Cook Time: ______ Cook Temp: ______

Ingredients:

Directions:

Notes:

Recipe:

Serves: Prep Time: Cook Time: Cook Temp:

Ingredients:

Directions:

Notes:

Recipe: ______________________________

Serves: __________ Prep Time: __________ Cook Time: __________ Cook Temp: __________

Ingredients:

Directions:

Notes:

Recipe:

Serves: Prep Time: Cook Time: Cook Temp:

Ingredients:

Directions:

Notes:

Recipe: ______________________

Serves: ________ Prep Time: ________ Cook Time: ________ Cook Temp: ________

Ingredients:

Directions:

Notes:

Recipe: ______

Serves: ______ Prep Time: ______ Cook Time: ______ Cook Temp: ______

Ingredients:

Directions:

Notes:

Recipe:

Serves: Prep Time: Cook Time: Cook Temp:

Ingredients:

Directions:

Notes:

Recipe:

Serves: Prep Time: Cook Time: Cook Temp:

Ingredients:

Directions:

Notes:

Recipe:

Serves: Prep Time: Cook Time: Cook Temp:

Ingredients:

Directions:

Notes:

Recipe:

Serves: Prep Time: Cook Time: Cook Temp:

Ingredients:

Directions:

Notes:

Recipe: ______________________________

Serves: ________ Prep Time: ________ Cook Time: ________ Cook Temp: ________

Ingredients:

Directions:

Notes:

Recipe: ______________________________

Serves: ________ Prep Time: ________ Cook Time: ________ Cook Temp: ________

Ingredients:

Directions:

Notes:

Recipe: __________

Serves: _____ Prep Time: _____ Cook Time: _____ Cook Temp: _____

Ingredients:

Directions:

Notes:

Recipe: ______________________________

Serves: ________ Prep Time: ________ Cook Time: ________ Cook Temp: ________

Ingredients:

Directions:

Notes:

Recipe: ____________________

Serves: ______ Prep Time: ______ Cook Time: ______ Cook Temp: ______

Ingredients:

Directions:

Notes:

Recipe:

Serves: Prep Time: Cook Time: Cook Temp:

Ingredients:

Directions:

Notes:

Recipe:

Serves: Prep Time: Cook Time: Cook Temp:

Ingredients:

Directions:

Notes:

Recipe:

Serves: Prep Time: Cook Time: Cook Temp:

Ingredients:

Directions:

Notes:

Recipe: ____________________

Serves: ________ Prep Time: ________ Cook Time: ________ Cook Temp: ________

Ingredients:

Directions:

Notes:

Recipe:

Serves: Prep Time: Cook Time: Cook Temp:

Ingredients:

Directions:

Notes:

Recipe:

Serves: Prep Time: Cook Time: Cook Temp:

Ingredients:

Directions:

Notes:

Recipe: ______________________________

Serves: ________ Prep Time: ________ Cook Time: ________ Cook Temp: ________

Ingredients:

Directions:

Notes:

Recipe: ____________________

Serves: ________ Prep Time: ________ Cook Time: ________ Cook Temp: ________

Ingredients:

Directions:

Notes:

Recipe: ____________________

Serves: ______ Prep Time: ______ Cook Time: ______ Cook Temp: ______

Ingredients:

Directions:

Notes:

Recipe:

Serves: Prep Time: Cook Time: Cook Temp:

Ingredients:

Directions:

Notes:

Recipe:

Serves: Prep Time: Cook Time: Cook Temp:

Ingredients:

Directions:

Notes:

Recipe:

Serves: Prep Time: Cook Time: Cook Temp:

Ingredients:

Directions:

Notes:

Recipe:

Serves: Prep Time: Cook Time: Cook Temp:

Ingredients:

Directions:

Notes:

Recipe:

Serves: Prep Time: Cook Time: Cook Temp:

Ingredients:

Directions:

Notes:

Recipe: ____________________

Serves: ________ Prep Time: ________ Cook Time: ________ Cook Temp: ________

Ingredients:

Directions:

Notes:

Recipe: ______

Serves: ______ Prep Time: ______ Cook Time: ______ Cook Temp: ______

Ingredients:

Directions:

Notes:

Recipe: ______

Serves: ______ Prep Time: ______ Cook Time: ______ Cook Temp: ______

Ingredients:

Directions:

Notes:

Recipe: ____________________

Serves: ________ Prep Time: ________ Cook Time: ________ Cook Temp: ________

Ingredients:

Directions:

Notes:

Recipe:

Serves: Prep Time: Cook Time: Cook Temp:

Ingredients:

Directions:

Notes:

Recipe: ______

Serves: ______ Prep Time: ______ Cook Time: ______ Cook Temp: ______

Ingredients:

Directions:

Notes:

Recipe:

Serves: Prep Time: Cook Time: Cook Temp:

Ingredients:

Directions:

Notes:

Recipe: ____________________

Serves: ______ Prep Time: ______ Cook Time: ______ Cook Temp: ______

Ingredients:

Directions:

Notes:

Recipe: ____________________

Serves: ________ Prep Time: ________ Cook Time: ________ Cook Temp: ________

Ingredients:

Directions:

Notes:

Recipe:

Serves: Prep Time: Cook Time: Cook Temp:

Ingredients:

Directions:

Notes:

Recipe:

Serves: Prep Time: Cook Time: Cook Temp:

Ingredients:

Directions:

Notes:

Recipe:

Serves: Prep Time: Cook Time: Cook Temp:

Ingredients:

Directions:

Notes:

Recipe: ____________________

Serves: ________ Prep Time: ________ Cook Time: ________ Cook Temp: ________

Ingredients:

Directions:

Notes:

Recipe: ______

Serves: ______ Prep Time: ______ Cook Time: ______ Cook Temp: ______

Ingredients:

Directions:

Notes:

Recipe:

Serves: Prep Time: Cook Time: Cook Temp:

Ingredients:

Directions:

Notes:

Recipe:

Serves:
Prep Time:
Cook Time:
Cook Temp:

Ingredients:

Directions:

Notes:

Recipe: ______

Serves: ______ Prep Time: ______ Cook Time: ______ Cook Temp: ______

Ingredients:

Directions:

Notes:

Made in the USA
Lexington, KY
04 December 2019

58137892R00057